Charlie's Trail

The Life and Art of C. M. Russell

Charlie's Trail

The Life and Art of C. M. Russell

by Gayle C. Shirley

TWODOT

A · TWODOT · BOOK

Co-published by Falcon Press Publishing and C.M. Russell Museum.
© 1996 by Falcon Press Publishing Co., Inc.
Helena and Billings, Montana

Text © 1996 C.M. Russell Museum
Great Falls, Montana
Published with assistance from the Malcolm S. "Bud" Mackay, Jr., Publication Fund.

Falcon Press gratefully acknowledges the assistance of Ginger Renner. The author wishes to
thank Jennifer Page for her research assistance. The C.M. Russell Museum wishes to thank
Elizabeth Dear, Nancy Wheeler, and Pam Hendrickson for their assistance. Special thanks to
Lori Bushly for managing this project.

Cover photo and art from the collection of the C.M. Russell Museum.
Border art from *Here's to all Old-Timers, Bob* (1911, C. M. Russell letter).
The epigraphs that begin each chapter are all quotes from Charlie Russell.

Design, typesetting, and other prepress work by Falcon Press, Helena, Montana.

Library of Congress Cataloging-in-Publication Data
Shirley, Gayle Corbett.
    Charlie's trail : the life and art of C. M. Russell / by Gayle C. Shirley
        p.   cm.
    "A Twodot book"—T.p. verso
    Includes index.
    Summary : Discusses the life and work of Charles Russell, painter,
sculptor, cowboy, and storyteller from Montana.
    ISBN 1-56044-410-X (hardcover). — ISBN 1-56044-444-4 (paperback)
    1. Russell, Charles M. (Charles Marion), 1864-1926—Juvenile
literature 2. Artists—United States—Biography—Juvenile
literature. 3. West (U.S.) in art—Juvenile literature. 4. West
(U.S.)—Description and travel—Juvenile literature. [1. Russell,
Charles M. (Charles Marion), 1864-1926 2. Artists. 3. West (U.S.)
in art. 4. Montana—Description and travel.]   I. Title.
N6537.R88S5 1996
709' .2—dc20
  [B]   95-51709
                                              CIP
                                               AC

The west
is dead my Friend
But writers hold the seed
And what they saw
Will live and grow
Again to those who read

C. M. Russell, 1917

List of Color Illustrations

Contents

Foreword

Charlie Russell was many things: a cowboy, a painter, a sculptor, a storyteller, and a friend to many. He loved the West, and he was fascinated by the diverse people who lived in the Big Sky Country. Living during a time of change, he felt a deep need to capture the images and stories of the vanishing West. He did so in his art, and he did it well.

Charlie had a deep interest in children and young people. He would invite them into his log studio, next to his house, in Great Falls, Montana. The studio was his home away from home and the place where he created his art. Young visitors were amazed by what they saw in Charlie's studio. There, he kept his oil paints, pencils, and the wax models of his sculptures, together with the cowboy gear and Indian outfits he would use as models for his art. Charlie welcomed his young friends, but while he was working, he would ask them to sit still and be quiet. When he took a break, he would entertain them by creating an animal—like a grizzly bear or a horse—out of wax, or he'd do Indian sign language with his hands, or he'd tell them a story about his days as a young cowboy.

Charlie Russell was a great storyteller, but his outstanding skills as an artist made him a true chronicler of the West. In this wonderfully written biography, author Gayle C. Shirley paints a colorful portrait of this great Western artist and captures his warm and playful spirit. Informative and easy to read, *Charlie's Trail: The Life and Art of C. M. Russell* is a splendid addition to any library.

Lorne E. Render, Director
C.M. Russell Museum
Great Falls, Montana

About Charlie's Spelling

Charlie Russell was a colorful and creative man. This is apparent not only in his art, but in his writing. In the many letters and stories he wrote, he often made spelling, grammar, and punctuation mistakes. Fortunately, that never stopped him from sharing his good-humored thoughts about life.

Throughout this book, when I've quoted Charlie, I've kept his original spelling and grammar. But sometimes I've corrected his punctuation, when his writing is otherwise hard to understand.

Charlie may have had a better grasp of English than his letters and books imply. But he liked the folksy lingo of the cowboy. He may have intentionally misspelled and misused words to give his yarns more color. By doing so, he preserved for us the sounds, as well as the sights, of the Old West.

Frisky
as a Colt

"I was a wild young man, but age has made me gentle."

The foreman of the brickyard was not amused. Someone had made an unflattering clay model of his head and left it where everyone was sure to see it. The other workers could hardly keep from snickering when they saw him.

The outraged foreman must have guessed right away who the culprit was. It was that mischievous ten-year-old, Charlie Russell. He was always charging through the grounds on his pony, Gyp, whooping like an Indian. Everyone knew he liked to make things out of clay.

History books don't tell us the outcome of this incident, which took place in Missouri in 1874. But it's easy to imagine the foreman squashing that sculpture until there was nothing left of it but a shapeless blob. He might have reacted differently if he could have foreseen the future. That rascal Russell was going to be a famous artist one day. The boy known for his creative pranks would grow into a man known for his artistic vision. He would capture in painting and sculpture the adventure and romance of the Old West—at a time when the Old West was fast becoming a memory.

J. Frank Dobie, a western writer and historian, would one day call Charlie Russell "the greatest painter that ever painted a range man, a range cow, a range horse, or a Plains Indian." The time would come when a single piece of Charlie's art would be worth a million dollars. One of his paintings would even hang in the White House.

Charlie's enthusiasm for art surfaced within a few years of his birth on March 19, 1864. He grew up on the family estate on the outskirts of St. Louis, along with four brothers and a sister. His parents, Mary Elizabeth Mead and Charles Silas Russell, were prosperous and influential members of their community. They made their living from farming, coal mining, and the manufacture of brick and tile. Although Charlie's full name was Charles Marion Russell, his family usually called him Chas, so as not to confuse him with his father.

One of Charlie's earliest memories was of a spanking he got for drawing pictures on the front stairs. Then, when he was only four years old, he got in trouble for wandering away from home. Fascinated by animals, he had tagged along after a man with a trained bear. When his frantic parents finally found him and carted him back home, Charlie scraped the mud from the soles of his boots and made a tiny bear of his own.

Throughout his life, Charlie would keep a lump of clay or beeswax in his pocket. While chatting with friends, he would

Charlie Russell was about four years old when he posed for this picture. He was
already a budding artist, but his talent wasn't always appreciated. He was not,
for example, admired for his drawings on the stairs in his family home.

C.M. RUSSELL MUSEUM, GREAT FALLS, MONTANA

13

absentmindedly model a tiny figure—maybe a pig, a horse, or a buffalo. Then he would mash it out with his thumb and start all over again. Sometimes he used hairs from a paintbrush to make manes and tails for his creations. As a youngster, he also carved animals out of soap and big potatoes.

Charlie apparently inherited his artistic talent from his mother. She had a good reputation as a painter in St. Louis, and she encouraged him to paint, sketch, and sculpt. By the time he was twelve, he was talented enough to win a blue ribbon for one of his drawings at the St. Louis County Fair.

From his father's side of the family, Charlie got his independent spirit and a passion for adventure. He grew up hearing stories of his daring relatives, who had been among the first white Americans to venture into the new frontier. His great-grandfather, Silas Bent, had been chief surveyor of Louisiana Territory after Lewis and Clark explored it. William Bent, Silas' son, had built the famous fur-trading post Bent's Fort on the Santa Fe Trail in what is now Colorado. Another of Silas' sons, Charles, had been killed by Pueblo Indians while he was governor of New Mexico Territory. And one of Charlie's uncles, William Fulkerson, had been a Pony Express rider. It was he who taught Charlie to ride and inspired his love of horses.

Charlie was fascinated with the romantic vision of the Wild West that all these stories inspired. He would gaze at the portrait of William Bent that hung in the Russell home and dream of following in the fur trader's footsteps. When his parents gave him a pony, he imagined himself a cowboy. He roped make-believe cattle and chased imaginary Indians. With his brothers, he played "massacre" and "scalped" his sister's dolls.

As much as he loved art and the West, Charlie hated school. It wasn't that he couldn't master reading, writing, and arithmetic. It was just that he had other, more tempting things on his mind.

School Boys and Teacher, ca. 1922, pen and ink.
C.M. RUSSELL MUSEUM, GREAT FALLS, MONTANA

His teachers often whipped and scolded him for daydreaming and for sketching animals and Indians in the margins of his books. Sometimes he would fashion figures out of clay that he dug from a nearby creek bed. He learned to model the clay under his desktop where neither he nor the teacher could see it.

Charlie found ways to get even with his teachers for the harsh punishments they gave him. One especially satisfying prank involved a teacher who liked to sit with his chair tilted back against a latched door behind him. The door led down a few steps to a storeroom. One day, Charlie secretly unlatched it but pushed it almost closed. The next time the teacher tipped back, he kept right on going down the stairs and landed headfirst in a pile of desks. Apparently, Charlie got away with the stunt.

It wasn't long before Charlie began playing hooky from school—often for days at a time. He would sneak down to the

15

docks along the Mississippi River to listen to the tall tales of the rivermen, fur traders, and mountain men. Although his parents were patient with their son's rebellious ways, they soon began to worry about his terrible grades. They didn't mind him dreaming about the West, but they expected him to get a good education so he could take over the family business one day.

When Charlie was fifteen, the Russells enrolled him in a military school in Burlington, New Jersey. They hoped he would learn to be more responsible about his studies and serious about his future. Instead, he traded drawings for homework. He spent hours on guard duty as punishment for breaking the rules. When he went home at the end of his first semester, school officials advised him not to come back. That was okay with Charlie. He would rather go west.

Next, Charlie's parents tried enrolling him in a local art school. They had always thought of art as a hobby, not a way to earn a living. But what else could they do? Imagine their surprise and disappointment when Charlie quit in disgust after only three days. He had spent the whole time having to draw a plaster foot, and the instructor had never been satisfied with his efforts.

Finally, Charlie's parents agreed to let him follow his dream. In 1880, they arranged for him to travel to Montana Territory with Wallis "Pike" Miller, a family friend who was part-owner of a sheep ranch there. Charlie was going to spend the summer working on the ranch. His parents thought he would find frontier life tougher than he had imagined. He would get this silly notion out of his head and rush back to civilization and the comforts of home.

But the Russells didn't realize the depth of their son's desire. ∩

Wild and Woollies

"Sheep and I did not get along very well."

The present Charlie's parents gave him for his sixteenth birthday was probably the best one he ever got. They bought him a railway ticket to Montana. In March 1880, he boarded a train with Pike Miller and chugged off across the Great Plains in a billow of coal black smoke. He was finally on his way to the land of the cowboy!

Montana Territory was mostly wilderness when Charlie arrived more than a century ago. It wouldn't become a state for another nine years. The rail line Charlie and Pike traveled had only recently crept its way north from Idaho and edged across the territorial border. So the two Missourians had to climb off at Red Rock, a scattering of tents and shacks at the end of the line in Montana's southwest corner.

The second leg of the journey was even more exciting. Charlie and Pike climbed into a stagecoach bound for Helena, the territorial capital. Charlie got to perch up top with the whip-cracking driver. They jounced along dim wagon trails, scanning the sage and juniper for coyotes, antelope, and buffalo. Charlie had never seen mountains as magnificent as the hazy blue Rockies that loomed to the west.

The stagecoach driver could tell that Charlie was a greenhorn. He figured he'd play a little joke on this eager and gullible kid. He warned Charlie not to tell anyone in Helena that he was from Missouri. They hang people from Missouri, he joshed, trying to keep a straight face. Wide-eyed Charlie believed every word and never dared tell a soul.

In 1880, Helena was a booming gold-mining camp of almost four thousand people. In two more years, it would be the first city in Montana to get electric lights. The next year, in 1883, the railroad would arrive, and the last stagecoach would rattle through Last Chance Gulch wrapped in bunting of red, white, and blue.

Charlie was awed by all the miners, mule skinners, mountain men, and bullwhackers crowding Helena's streets. And he was startled to see Indians wandering freely through town. Only four years had passed since Custer and most of his Seventh Cavalry had perished at the Little Bighorn. Although there had been no major battles in the territory in recent years, there was still some friction between "red men" and whites. But it wasn't unusual for Indians to drift into town and peer with curiosity in cabin windows.

Pike and Charlie stayed in Helena just long enough to buy a wagon, horses, and supplies. Charlie purchased a mare and a gelding, but he wasn't very impressed with them. He eventually sold the mare and bought a brown and white pinto for forty-five dollars from some Blackfeet Indians. He named it Monte, and it

Charlie loved horses and owned several during his lifetime. His favorite was Monte
(shown above), a pinto he bought from the Blackfeet Indians soon after reaching
Montana. The pair were together for almost twenty-five years.

C.M. RUSSELL MUSEUM, GREAT FALLS, MONTANA

19

would be his companion for many years to come.

While in Helena, Charlie outfitted himself as a cowboy, with a big-brimmed hat, a buckskin shirt, and high-heeled boots. He personalized his get-up by tying a red French Canadian sash around his waist. He would wear a similar sash for the rest of his life—even on formal occasions.

Almost two hundred miles lay between Helena and Pike's ranch in central Montana. So the pair set out across broken prairie and through the Big Belt and Castle mountains. Charlie let his imagination fill the empty country with visions of adventure. He was riding along the Musselshell River—well ahead of Pike— when shouts shattered his daydreams. Crow Indians were galloping toward him, shrieking and firing their rifles into the air. Charlie was terrified! Was he going to lose his scalp so soon after reaching Montana?

When the Crows got close, the chief reined his horse and peered into Charlie's face. "White papoose much afraid?" he teased. This was the Indians' idea of a joke! The chief went on to warn Charlie that he shouldn't ride so far ahead of his companion. This was Blackfeet country, the warrior explained, and "they have bad hearts." When the Crows finally rode away, Charlie was able to breathe again. Little did he know that one day he would look forward to the company of Indians.

About a month after leaving St. Louis, Charlie and his companion arrived cold and travel weary at Pike's sheep ranch in the Judith Basin. A heavy, spring snow had made the last few miles of the trip an ordeal. But to Charlie, central Montana was like a western Garden of Eden. He later described part of it like this:

> Shut off from the outside world, it was a hunter's paradise, bounded by walls of mountains and containing miles of grassy open spaces, more green and beautiful than

Before the White Man Came, ca. 1922, pen and ink and graphite.
AMON CARTER MUSEUM (1961.318), FORT WORTH, TEXAS.

any man-made parks. These parks and the mountains behind them swarmed with deer, elk, mountain sheep, and bear, besides beaver and other small fur-bearing animals. The creeks were alive with trout. Nature had surely done her best, and no king of the old times could have claimed a more beautiful and bountiful domain.

Charlie was not nearly so enthusiastic about his new job. He wanted to be a rowdy cowboy, not a lazy sheepherder. When Pike told him to take some sheep to yonder hill and watch them, Charlie carried his art supplies along to keep from getting bored. While the flock grazed, he sketched and painted, totally absorbed in his work. When at last he looked up to check on his charges, the woollies had wandered away. Pike was disgusted with "that ornery kid Russell." It wasn't long before the two parted ways.

Charlie rode into nearby Utica to see if he could get a job tending horses. But the folks at the stage station there had heard

about his disastrous attempts at sheepherding. So naturally they weren't about to trust him with their mounts.

Charlie didn't know what to do next. Here he was, thousands of miles from home, with no shelter, no food, no job, and no friends. Luckily for him, fate was about to grab his reins and lead him down the right trail.

Charlie was camped along the Judith River, reluctantly making plans to go home, when a mountain man set up his own camp not far away. He looked as tough and independent as the characters Charlie had imagined while reading boyhood adventure novels. The fellow's name was Jake Hoover. He worked as a trapper and hunter, supplying meat to ranchers and miners in the area.

The man strolled into Charlie's meager camp, looked around, and asked, "Where do you keep your grub?"

"I ain't got none," Charlie grumbled. His situation had put him in a grumpy mood. So Jake offered to share some fresh elk meat with him.

Encouraged by the older man's generosity, Charlie poured out his troubles. He told Jake about his lifelong dream to come west and be a cowboy. Jake was sympathetic. He had come to Montana himself when he was only sixteen years old, to look for a brother who was prospecting for gold. He knew how hard it could be to survive in the wilderness. So he invited Charlie to share his cabin for a spell, at least until the kid could find a job.

For about two years, Charlie helped Jake with his chores and hunting, delighting in the mountain man's footloose way of life. "He had no more fear of a bear than I would have of a milk cow," Charlie said of the tough old hunter. But he also recognized that Jake had a sentimental side. Years later, he referred to it in a tale he told his friends:

You could see deer from the door of his shack 'most any day. But do you think he would kill a deer that stuck about his shack? No, sir, he'd as soon take a shot at men as kill one of them deer. An' I've seen the time when there wasn't enough grub in that shack to bait a mousetrap, too. Every livin' thing around there liked old Jake. Pine squirrels would climb into his lap an' sit on his shoulder. Chickadees were dead stuck on him; they'd pick crumbs from his lips an' he always fed 'em plenty.

Although Charlie's story probably grew in the retelling, he was clearly fond of the mountain man. Jake felt the same way about Charlie. He was also impressed with the young artist's talent, but he could be a tough critic. He made Charlie paint his pictures of animals over and over until he got them exactly right. He showed Charlie the salt lick he had set out near his cabin, and the boy sat hidden nearby for hours, sketching the animals that came to feed. Charlie also helped Jake skin his game and learned a lot about animal anatomy. The knowledge would help to make him a better wildlife artist.

Finally, after two years with Jake, Charlie decided it was time to say good-bye. The two had developed a lasting friendship. But Charlie had finally saved enough money to go home, and he knew his family was eager to see him. ∩

A Home
on the Range

*"Old Ma Nature was kind to her red children
and the old time cow puncher was her adopted son."*

Charlie enjoyed the visit with his family and the welcome-home parties they gave. But in only a few weeks, he got tired of the bustle of the city. To his parents' dismay, he decided to return to the place he now thought of as home: the vast mountains and prairies of faraway Montana.

This time, Charlie traveled west with his cousin, Jim Fulkerson. The two eighteen-year-olds took the train to Billings, Montana Territory. They planned to ride horseback the remaining 150 miles to Hoover's cabin. But while they were still in the city shopping for supplies, Jim came down with Rocky Mountain spotted fever. Two weeks later, he died, and Charlie headed out alone with only fifty cents in his pocket.

Plodding northward through a wet spring snow, Charlie met a cattle outfit that was looking for a wrangler. To his delight, the boss hired him. His job was to tend the hundreds of saddle horses that the cowboys rode during roundup.

"It was a lucky thing no one knew me or I'd never got the job. . . ," he wrote later. "I was considered worthless [among sheepherders] and was spoken of as 'that ornery kid Russell,' but not among cowmen."

Charlie still wasn't quite a full-fledged cowboy. He didn't bust broncs or rope and brand cattle. But he figured he was close enough. At last, he was riding the open range through the dust kicked up by countless hooves. He fell asleep to the howl of wolves and the lowing of the longhorns, and, at branding time, he breathed the stink of burning hair and flesh. As far as Charlie was concerned, this was heaven.

In the fall, when the cattle were driven to the nearest railroad for shipment to market, Charlie hired on as a "nighthawk" for a group of ranchers in the Judith Basin. In those days before barbed-wire fences, his job was to ride around the cattle at night, keeping them calm and together. The work was often pleasant and peaceful. He sang to the sleepy animals and gazed in wonder at the stars. But it could be dangerous, too. Any little noise or movement could spook the longhorns and trigger a stampede. The nighthawk would have to gallop blindly through the dark, trying to stop the panicky cattle. Imagine racing across the prairie when you can't see where you're going! If your horse stepped in a gopher hole or off the edge of an embankment, you could fly out of your saddle like an arrow from a bow. If you were lucky, you might come away with nothing more than bruises. If you

weren't, you might go to your grave with a broken neck.

For the next eleven years, Charlie sang to horses and cattle. "I was neither a good roper nor rider," he would later say. "I was a night wrangler. How good I was, I'll leave it for the people I worked for to say. . . . In the spring I wrangled horses, in the fall I herded beef. I worked for the big outfits and always held my job."

Because he worked at night, Charlie was able to spend part of each day painting the scenes around him. He would stretch out on his belly under a wagon in the shade and sketch the cowboys at work and play. Since paper and canvas were hard to come by, he painted on anything else he could find, including cracker boxes, birch bark, and buckskin. When he wasn't using his paints and brushes, he stowed them in an old sock that he hung from his saddle horn.

Many of Charlie's paintings are of events he witnessed during his cowboy years. He was a careful observer who tried hard to paint even the smallest details correctly—right down to the brands on the cattle and the horses. He especially was impressed with the risky job of roping. Several of his pictures show how things can go wrong when a cowboy's lariat goes astray. Charlie practiced roping for most of his life, if only for fun and exercise.

Many of the cowboys Charlie got to know were as plucky as the heroes he had imagined as a boy. Many of them had an equally good impression of him. They fondly called him "Kid" Russell, since he was younger than most of the crew. And according to one of them, they would "hurry in at night just to listen to his yarns and laugh at the pictures he drew." Charlie often gave his sketches and paintings away to anyone who admired them, and the men proudly hung them on the bunkhouse walls.

By his early twenties, Charlie had a reputation as a gifted Western artist—at least among the residents of Montana Territory. During the summer and winter, between spring roundups and fall trail drives, he spent much of his time in the back room of a Utica saloon. The owner had let him use it as his first art studio.

That same saloonkeeper gave Charlie his first formal commission: to paint a picture to hang behind the bar. Since Charlie had a hard time finding any canvas, he used a smooth pine board almost seven feet long and a foot and a half wide. On it, he painted *Western Scene*—a three-part picture of Indians attacking a wagon train, elk, and antelope. It was crude and amateurish compared to the masterpieces that would follow, but the saloonkeeper must have been satisfied. Two years later, he commissioned another painting. This time, Charlie created a panoramic view of a cattle roundup near Utica. The Judith Basin cowboys loved it. They could recognize every man and horse.

Charlie had painted the Utica roundup crew before, in a piece he called *Breaking Camp*. Finished in 1885 when he was only twenty-one, it was the largest oil painting he had done so far. Without telling anyone, he sent it home to his mother and asked her to enter it in the St. Louis Art Exposition of 1886. This was the first time one of Charlie's paintings was displayed outside Montana.

A year later, the *Helena Weekly Herald* reported that his oils and watercolors had "found their way to the centers of population" and were adorning "the offices and homes of wealthy citizens of Montana's principal cities." That same year, the Helena *Independent* first called him "the Cowboy Artist." The nickname would stick with him for the rest of his life.

While Charlie's fortunes as an artist were changing for the better, the glory days of the cowboy were nearing a disastrous end. In the fall of 1886, hundreds of thousands of cattle crowded the range in Montana. The year had been unusually dry, so the grass was sparse and withered. With such a skimpy food supply,

Charlie always considered his cowboy days some of the best times in his life. In approximately 1882, when this picture was taken, he was a wrangler for a roundup crew in central Montana. He's the third man from the left in the front row. The rest of the cowboys called him "Kid Russell" because he was younger than most of them.

C.M. RUSSELL MUSEUM, GREAT FALLS, MONTANA

the livestock would be lucky to make it through the winter.

Then, in November, a blizzard raged out of the north and dumped a heavy load of snow. According to the Fort Benton *River Press*, the wind was so strong "the cattle had to tie their tails to their hind legs to prevent them being blown off." In December, a brief warm spell brought a welcome thaw. But temperatures soon tumbled again and created a thick cover of ice over the range. Hungry longhorns gashed their noses and legs as they tried to break through it to graze.

Historian Joseph Kinsey Howard vividly described the tragedy in his book *Montana: High, Wide, and Handsome*:

> Half dead from cold and hunger, their bodies covered with sores and frozen blood, bewildered and blind in a world of impenetrable white, [the cattle] blundered into the barbed-wire fences, crumpled against them, and perished. . . .
>
> As the storms and cold continued . . . the tragedy of the range was brought into the towns. Starving cattle staggered through village streets, collapsed and died in dooryards. Five thousand head invaded the outskirts of the newborn city of Great Falls, bawling for food. They snatched up the saplings the proud city had just planted, [and] gorged themselves upon garbage.

The next two months offered no relief. Some ranches recorded temperatures as low as sixty degrees below zero. Cowboys were describing the winter as "hell without the heat."

Finally, in March, warm chinook winds melted the snow, and ranchers rode out to check on their herds. What they found made them sick. Tens of thousands of cattle had died in what would be known thereafter as the "Hard Winter." Their rotting

carcasses littered the plains and foothills. Cattlemen had learned a hard lesson. From now on, they would fence the range so they could find their livestock more easily and provide the animals with food and shelter. The days of the open range were over. The end of the great cowboy era would not be far behind.

Charlie spent that winter at the OH Ranch near Utica. A Helena cattleman, Louis Kaufman, was wintering his longhorns there. When he wrote to ask the ranch foreman how his herd was faring, Russell responded by painting a postcard-sized watercolor. It showed a gaunt steer, knee-deep in snow and surrounded by hungry wolves. He called it *Waiting for a Chinook*, and it told the story of that brutal winter better than words ever could.

The owner of the OH Ranch sent the painting to Kaufman. Soon, it appeared in newspapers across the country, to illustrate stories of the terrible losses suffered by ranchers that year. Today, that sad little watercolor remains Charlie's most famous work of art. Ω

Among 'Red Brothers'

"The Red man was the true American
They have almost gon. but will never be forgotten."

Two decades before Charlie came to Montana, millions of buffalo roamed the grasslands of the West. By the time he reached Red Rock in 1880, the great herds were nearly gone—the victims of greedy hide hunters and thrill-seeking "sportsmen" who sometimes shot the beasts by the dozens and left them to rot in the sun. Large herds of cattle were beginning to take their place.

To the Plains Indians, the buffalo had been "the great giver," the provider of almost everything they needed to survive. The animal was more than just the staple of their diet. They used its

hide to make blankets, clothes, and tepees. They used its horns to make tools, its sinew to make thread, its bladder to make drinking jugs, and its hooves to make glue. They even used its dried dung as a substitute for firewood.

The Plains Indians suffered as the buffalo disappeared. They no longer had the strength to resist the U.S. government as it chopped their once great hunting grounds into reservations. Forced to give up their wandering way of life, they had to depend on beef handed out by government agents. Often, there wasn't enough to go around, and thousands of Indians starved.

To Russell, the buffalo was "one of natures biggest gifts," and the Indian was the "true American." He considered them important symbols of the Wild West. Alarmed by their decline, he resolved to preserve them on canvas before they were lost forever.

In May of 1888, Charlie headed north to Canada to spend the summer loafing and visiting friends. During his stay, he had almost daily contact with the Indian tribes of the region, including the Blackfoot, Sarsi, and Assiniboine. The time he spent in the lodges of his "red brothers" gave him an excellent chance to learn firsthand about the Indians' way of life. It also gave him an edge over other Western artists. It helped him to paint the Indians with greater expertise.

The Blackfoot tribes welcomed Charlie into their villages. They taught him sign language and called him Ah-Wah-Cous, which in their language meant "antelope." Charlie had stitched a patch of buckskin onto the seat of his pants to keep them from wearing out in the saddle. It reminded the Blackfoot people of the antelope's white rump.

Charlie grew to love the simple ways of the Indians. He admired their playfulness, their honesty, and their respect for nature. "Man for man, an Injun's as good as a white man any

Charlie respected Indians' love of nature and admired their sense of humor. He often made them the subject of his paintings, and he counted many of them among his friends. He's shown here with Big Belly and his wife during a 1920 visit to Canada.

C.M. RUSSELL MUSEUM, GREAT FALLS, MONTANA

day," he once wrote. "No Injun ever did me dirt an' many a one's done me favors. When he's a good friend, he's the best friend in the world."

So far, Charlie had been best known for his paintings of cowboy scenes. Now, he began to paint Indians more than any other subject. He tended to idealize them, portraying them as dignified "noblemen of the prairies." But he also was one of only a few artists to paint them in their tepees, involved in the routines of their daily lives. In *The Beauty Parlor*, he painted a touching domestic scene of a Blackfoot woman braiding her husband's hair. With artwork like this, he hoped to convince other whites that Indians weren't all "savages" who were constantly on the warpath. They were human beings capable of tender emotions.

Charlie respected the Indians' customs and was ashamed of the way the white man had cheated them of their lands. In a letter to a friend, he wrote, "This is the onley real American. He fought an' died for his country. to day he has no vote, no country and is not a citizen, but history will not forget him."

After Charlie's return from Canada, his reputation as an artist continued to grow. Montana newspapers praised his work and published reproductions of his paintings. A New York magazine called him "one of the best animal painters in the world." And, in 1890, he published his first book, *Studies of Western Life*. It was a collection of black-and-white reproductions of twelve of his early oils.

Despite all this favorable recognition, Charlie continued to work as a cowboy until 1893. After that, he never sang to cattle again. But he would never forget those carefree days and nights on the open range. He would always consider his time as a cowboy one of the most fulfilling chapters of his life.

Charlie's last job as a cowboy was to accompany a train full of cattle to market in Chicago in the fall of 1893. He was

Mothers Under the Skin, 1900, pen and ink.
C.M. RUSSELL MUSEUM, GREAT FALLS, MONTANA

Last of His Race, 1899, pen and ink.
C.M. RUSSELL MUSEUM, GREAT FALLS, MONTANA

By the time he posed for this picture in about 1890, Charlie had an excellent
reputation as an artist—at least among the people of Montana. But
it wasn't until 1893 that he had the courage to hang up his saddle
and try making a living with his paintbrush.

C.M. RUSSELL MUSEUM, GREAT FALLS, MONTANA

unimpressed with the sooty railroad yards and belching factories of the city. "If I had a winter home in Hell and a summer home in Chicago, I think I'd spend my summers at my winter home," he wrote to a friend. "There might be more people there but there couldent be more smoke."

He did enjoy spending a few days exploring the Chicago World's Fair. Then he headed south to see his family in Missouri.

While in St. Louis, Charlie paid a visit to William Niedringhaus, a prominent local businessman who also owned ranches in Montana. One of them, the N Bar N, had hired Charlie on a number of occasions. Now, Niedringhaus commissioned him to paint several scenes of ranch life.

It was this commission that gave Charlie the courage to hang up his spurs and pick up his paintbrush full-time. He knew that if he were going to make a living as an artist, he would have to buckle down to work. So he moved from Great Falls to Cascade, a small town about twenty-five miles to the southwest. He thought there might be fewer distractions there. He set up a studio in a vacant courtroom and eventually produced more than fifteen paintings for Niedringhaus.

Charlie was shy about pricing his work. He once said anyone who would buy one of his paintings had to be a "sucker." He rarely asked more than twenty-five dollars, and he often simply traded his art for grub or other necessities. He also continued to give it away to his growing legion of friends.

As Charlie finished each painting for Niedringhaus, he asked a chum, Vin Fortune, to wrap and mail it—and to write a letter telling how much it cost. Fortune thought the prices that Charlie named were pitiful. So he secretly doubled them. Charlie was baffled when the money arrived, but Fortune convinced him that Niedringhaus must be so pleased with Charlie's work that he decided to double the artist's fee.

Throughout 1893 and 1894, Charlie kept his nose to his easel. He completed more than forty watercolors and twenty oils. By 1895, he needed a little vacation. He also needed a business manager who recognized the value of his work and demanded the prices it deserved.

He was about to find one—right there in tiny Cascade. ∩

Gettin' Hitched

"She took me for better or worse
and I will leave it to her which she got."

Charlie's whole life was about to change course—and all because of a dinner invitation.

As a bachelor and a struggling artist, he wasn't about to turn down the offer of a good, home-cooked meal. So when an old friend, Ben Roberts, suggested he come over for dinner one evening in October 1895, Charlie naturally said yes. He'd been a guest at the Roberts home in Cascade many times before. He knew he could count on good company and a meal that would stretch his belly.

Charlie breezed into the Roberts' kitchen and stopped dead

in his tracks. There was a new fixture in the Roberts home—and a mighty pretty one at that. As he stood there tongue-tied, Mrs. Roberts introduced him to the newest member of the household: a sweet-faced seventeen-year-old by the name of Nancy Cooper. She had recently come to live with the Robertses to do housework and care for their children.

Charlie was enchanted. For the rest of the evening, he was more outgoing than usual, amusing his hosts with tales of the good old days. Nancy was obviously attracted to the sturdy, middle-aged cowboy. Years later, she described her first impression of him:

> The picture that is engraved on my memory of him is of a man a little above average height and weight, wearing a soft shirt, a Stetson hat on the back of his blonde head, tight trousers, held up by a "half-breed sash" that clung just above the hip bones, [and] high-heeled riding boots on very small, arched feet. His face was Indian-like, square jaw and chin, large mouth, tightly closed firm lips . . , straight nose, high cheek bones, gray-blue deep-set eyes that seemed to see everything, but with an expression of honesty and understanding. . . . His hands were good-sized, perfectly shaped, with long, slender fingers. . . . When he talked, he used them a lot to emphasize what he was saying, much as an Indian would do.

Charlie began spending a lot of time at the Roberts home. In the evenings, he and Nancy would stroll hand in hand along the banks of the Missouri River. He proved just how much he liked her when he gave her his favorite horse, Monte. His friends were shocked. "That settles it," one of them remarked. "A man don't give a gal his hoss—not a man like Russ anyhow—'less he's

The Buffalo Hunt, No. 39, 1919, oil on canvas, Amon Carter Museum (1961.146), Fort Worth, Texas

When Wagon Trails Were Dim, 1919, oil,
The National Cowboy Hall of Fame and Western Heritage Center, Oklahoma City, Oklahoma

Innocent Allies, 1913, oil, The Thomas Gilcrease Institute of American History and Art (0137.2324), Tulsa, Oklahoma

In Without Knocking, 1909, oil on canvas, Amon Carter Museum (1961.201), Fort Worth, Texas

Man's Weapons Are Useless When Nature Goes Armed, 1916, oil on canvas, Sid Richardson Collection of Western Art, Fort Worth, Texas

Indians Crossing the Plains, 1902, watercolor, Eiteljorg Museum of American Indians and Western Art, Indianapolis, Indiana

Beauty Parlor, 1907, watercolor, C.M. Russell Museum, Great Falls, Montana

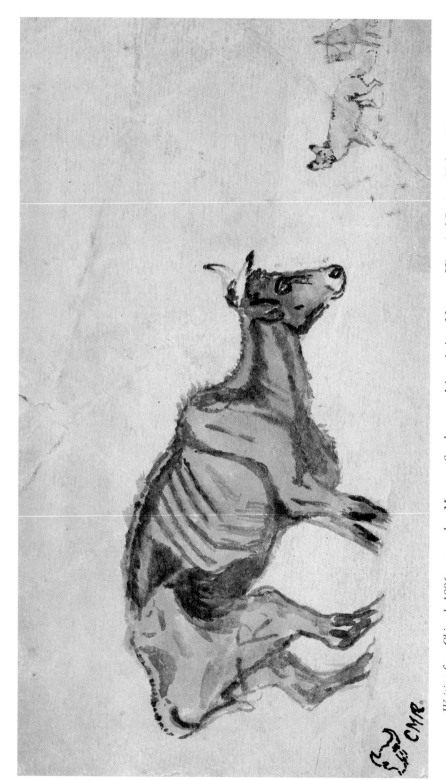

Waiting for a Chinook, 1886, watercolor, Montana Stockgrowers' Association, Montana Historical Society, Helena, Montana

plumb locoed 'bout her. He'll have to marry the gal now to git his hoss back."

But plenty of people were warning the pair not to marry. The local doctor told Charlie that Nancy had frequent fainting spells. He suspected she had a bad heart and would die within three years.

Folks reminded Nancy that Charlie was fourteen years older than her. He was a footloose bachelor who was probably set in his ways. And he'd never managed to make a decent living for himself. How was he supposed to provide for her?

But by now, Charlie and Nancy were too fond of each other to care what other people thought. Eventually, he asked her to marry him. His nephew Austin Russell described the momentous occasion:

> It took Charlie months to make up his mind, and when he finally asked Nancy she refused. He took her for a walk at sunset, they went down by the river and crossed the echoing, wooden bridge, and on the bridge he proposed, and she said No.
>
> Years afterward, he made a little watercolor of it—an autumn evening, the sky darkening to night, a cold wind blowing and they have just left the bridge. Nancy, downcast, is walking in front with her hands in a muff, her coat buttoned up tight and a little black hat on her head. Charlie following close behind with his coat blown open and sash and white shirt showing . . . his arms extended in a pleading, persuading, arguing gesture, his hat on the back of his head. That's all there is to it; not much of a picture, but it tells the story.
>
> In the end, of course, she said Yes.

Charlie's life changed course in 1896, when he married Nancy Cooper. She got him to take his art seriously and found new buyers for his work. People called her "the Robber" because she demanded such high prices for his paintings. But Charlie considered her "the best booster and pardner a man ever had." He once said, "If she hadn't prodded me, I wouldn't have done the work I did."

C.M. RUSSELL MUSEUM, GREAT FALLS, MONTANA

Charlie and Nancy were married at twilight on September 9, 1896, in the parlor of the Roberts home. Charlie slicked himself up for the occasion. Nancy wore a blue wedding gown that Mrs. Roberts had helped her make. Around her neck, she wore a string of blue beads—a wedding gift from Charlie.

After the ceremony, the handful of guests celebrated with cake and ice cream. The newlyweds set up housekeeping in a one-room shack that belonged to the Robertses and wasn't far from their home. According to Nancy, they started life together with only seventy-five dollars between them.

Despite everybody's reservations, Mr. and Mrs. Charles M. Russell remained devoted to one another for the next thirty years. And Mamie, as Charlie called his wife, had a big impact on his artistic career. He later acknowledged, "The lady I trotted in double harness with was the best booster an' pardner a man ever had. . . . If it hadn't been for Mamie I wouldn't have a roof over my head."

About a year after their wedding, Nancy persuaded Charlie to move to Great Falls, where there were more people to buy his paintings. A few years later, the couple built a respectable, two-story house in the most fashionable part of town. They paid for it with money Charlie's mother had left him when she died. Later, in 1903, they would construct an art studio next door. Built with telephone poles, it was designed to remind Charlie of Jake Hoover's cabin.

One day, Charles Schatzlein, a friend who owned an art gallery in Butte, stopped by the Russell home with a profitable idea. Nancy later recalled the man's advice:

"Do you know, Russell," he said, "you don't ask enough for your pictures. That last bunch you sent me, I sold one for enough to pay for six. I am paying you your

For several years, Charlie painted in the parlor of the Russell home in Great Falls,
Montana. Nancy didn't like the mess, so in 1903 they built a log studio next
door to the house. Charlie spent many hours there, entertaining friends as
well as working. He also filled it with things that served as models for
his paintings, including this collection of real Indian clothing.

C.M. RUSSELL MUSEUM, GREAT FALLS, MONTANA

price, but it's not enough. I think your wife should take hold of that end of the game and help you out."

From that time, the prices of Charlie's work began to advance until it was possible to live a little more comfortably.

Before Nancy and Charlie were married, he was lucky to get fifty dollars for a painting. That seemed like plenty to him. After all, it was a whole month's wages for a cowboy. But in only a few years, Nancy was selling his works for several hundred dollars apiece.

Charlie admitted to friends that he was embarrassed by her boldness and shocked when people paid the high prices she asked. But he also had to admit that his reputation was growing. Schatzlein had judged correctly. Charlie had the soft heart, but Nancy had the head for business.

She was "as smart as a steel trap and as quick as the lash of a whip," Austin Russell claimed. "Nancy got action out of everyone around her. Nobody could accuse her of driving Charlie, but without her he would have amounted to very little."

Much to Charlie's sorrow, the Russells never had children of their own. In 1916, when he was fifty-two and Nancy thirty-eight, they adopted an infant they named Jack. Charlie adored children and often entertained the neighborhood kids with rip-roaring stories of the Wild West. Now, he pampered his new son. He pushed him up and down the street in his baby carriage and bragged about him to passersby. Charlie had always longed for the past, but now he had a link to the future. ∩

The Russell family is shown here in about 1925 at Bull Head Lodge, a summer
cabin they built on Lake McDonald. Still standing on its original location, the cabin
is located within the boundaries of Glacier National Park.

C.M. RUSSELL MUSEUM, GREAT FALLS, MONTANA

Picture Talk
and Paper Talk

*"Any man that can make a livin' doin'
what he likes is lucky—an' I'm that."*

Spurred on by Nancy, Charlie began to change from a cowboy who wanted to be an artist into an artist who used to be a cowboy. She insisted that he keep regular work hours so he could produce more paintings. Every day, he got up soon after sunrise, fed and watered his horse and chickens, took a cup of hot lemon-water to Nancy in bed, and cooked himself hotcakes, bacon, and coffee. Then he traipsed off to his studio to paint until noon.

"He did surprisingly little fumbling around waiting for inspiration," Austin Russell said. "He went right to work," usually

47

on two or three canvases at once. When he got stuck while working on one, he set it aside and focused on another. It took him about three months to complete a major oil painting.

After lunch, Charlie snatched a half-hour nap. Then he slapped on his Stetson, saddled his horse, and moseyed downtown to spend a few hours swapping yarns with his pals. To Charlie, friendship was even more important than work. "Good friends," he said, "make the roughest trail easy." But Nancy made sure he didn't let his socializing interfere with his art. If she found visitors in Charlie's studio while he was supposed to be working, she didn't hesitate to shoo them out.

In 1903, the Russells went by train to St. Louis. They wanted to arrange to have some of Charlie's artwork exhibited the following year at the St. Louis World's Fair. While they were in his hometown, Charlie had his first show at an art gallery. From Missouri, they went on to New York City, where an illustrator friend introduced Charlie to the art editors of several major magazines.

Charlie didn't like New York, or "the Big Camp," as he called it. "It is not for me," he said. "It's too big and there are too many tall tepees. I'd rather live in a place where I know somebody and where everybody is Somebody . . . . Down there you've got to be a millionaire to be anybody."

But the trip to New York did give Charlie's career a boost. He got a rush of orders to illustrate calendars, books, and magazine articles. Soon, he was one of the leading Western illustrators of his time. In fact, he always thought of himself as an illustrator rather than a "real" artist.

While he was in New York, Charlie created a sculpture that would become his first to be cast in bronze. Called *Smoking Up*, it was of a rollicking cowboy on a rearing horse firing his six-gun into the air. One of the five original castings was presented to

Smoking Up, modeled 1904.
C.M. RUSSELL MUSEUM, GREAT FALLS, MONTANA

President Theodore Roosevelt.

Charlie had been toying with sculpture all of his life—ever since, at the age of four, he had made that tiny bear. He often said he felt more comfortable sculpting than painting. He even used wax and clay figures as models in his studio. He would fashion little men and animals and pose them as he wanted them to appear in a painting. Then he would hang an electric light over them where he imagined the sun to be. The models would cast shadows on the ground and each other just as they would in real life. Charlie would then transfer the effect to canvas.

Always a colorful storyteller, Charlie began about this time to put some of his tales into writing. He found that his stories of the Wild West were almost as popular as his art—and probably for the same reasons. They were full of detail, suspense, humor, and a sentimental longing for what he called "the honest days"— the days of the open range.

At first, Charlie wrote short stories for magazines. Eventually, he published three story collections in book form: *Rawhide Rawlins Stories* (1921), *More Rawhides* (1925), and *Trails Plowed Under* (1927), a collection of the first two. He illustrated his books with lively pen-and-ink drawings.

Charlie also was a creative and amusing letter-writer. Often, he illustrated his correspondence with sketches or small watercolors that said as much or more than the words they accompanied. That extra effort helped make up for the fact that he wasn't very quick about responding to his mail. He started one note to a friend with "I got a letter from you about three years ago so I thought Id hurry up and answer it."

By now, Charlie's career was gathering speed like a tumbleweed in a tempest. In 1911, he had his first major one-man show in New York City. That same year, he won an important commission: to paint a mural for the Montana House

Friend Bob we
received the

and thank you very
much

we havent done a thing
with two of then

and hope to do as well
with the other pair
when you come to town dont
forget our latch string is
on the out side   your Friend C M Russell

Friend Bob (Thoroughman), 1899, illustrated letter, pen and ink
(Richard Flood Collection).
C.M. RUSSELL MUSEUM, GREAT FALLS, MONTANA

of Representatives. He had to raise the roof of his studio to fit the canvas inside. Twelve feet high and twenty-five feet wide, it was the largest painting he ever did. He called it *Lewis and Clark Meeting the Flathead Indians at Ross' Hole*, and many people considered it his masterpiece. It still hangs in the House Chambers of the state Capitol in Helena.

In 1914, Charlie gained international recognition with a successful show at an art gallery in London. The owners insisted that he wear a tuxedo on opening night. But Charlie balked, and the gallery people finally compromised. Charlie wore the tux—along with his cowboy boots and red sash.

To Nancy, the highlight of the trip was dinner at the castle of an English lord. She was delighted to be hobnobbing with such high society. The aristocrats were delighted with Charlie's down-to-earth tales.

Through Nancy's efforts, Charlie's work was exhibited in many major cities, including Boston, Chicago, San Francisco, Los Angeles, Winnipeg, Calgary, and Washington, D.C. Charlie would just as soon have stayed in Montana, or "God's country," as he called it. But, as he said, "If I depended on my home state for commissions and sales, I would starve."

As it was, Charlie eventually was able to get as much as ten thousand dollars for a single oil painting—"dead man's prices," as he put it. Typically, an artist's work goes up in value after he or she dies. When one of his paintings sold for that amount in 1921, it was reportedly the most anyone had ever paid for the work of a living American artist.

Charlie's work was and still is popular because it brims with tension and wit, and because it captures in glowing colors the romance and adventure of the Old West. Looking at one of his paintings is like looking through a rose-colored window into a simpler but more exciting time.

Gutzon Borglum, the sculptor who created Mount Rushmore, once said that "Russell had . . . the power to draw animals, horses, [and] cattlemen in the mixed-up, tangled-up situations daily occurring in the wild unfenced West—situations no other artist has ever attempted."

One art critic called him "the official historian of the West that has passed."

Despite his growing fame and fortune, Charlie remained a simple, modest man. He refused to take credit for his artistic genius. "Talent like birthmarks are gifts an' no credit nor fault of those who ware them," he said.

Charlie Russell painted and sculpted more than four thousand pieces of art in his lifetime—all without any formal art training. Instead, he said, "Ma Nature was my teacher. I'll leave it up to you whether she was a good one." ∩

Christmas at the Line Camp, 1917, watercolor (Trigg Collection).
C.M. RUSSELL MUSEUM, GREAT FALLS, MONTANA

Christmas at the Line Camp

Last night I drifted back in dreams
To Childhoods stamping ground
Im in my little bed it seems, the Old folks whispering round
My sox is hung - Maws tucked me in
Its Christmas Eave you see
Iv said my prayers blessed all my kin
Im good as good can be
But suddenly Im wakened wide
From out this youthfull dream
By jingling bells thats just out side
Hung on som restless team
Reminded by rumatic shin
And lumbagoed back thats sore

Whiskred face and hair that thin
I aint no kid no more
An getting my boots I open the door
An Im sum suprised to see
An old tim freighter I knowed before
But its years since he called on me
Hes an under sized skinner
Good natured and stout
With a teem like himself
All small
Its the same old Cuss
Maw tells me about
Just old Santy Claus raindeers and all
Hes a holding his ribbons like an old Timer would
When he nods his head to me
I wish youd put me right if you could
Im way off the trail says he
I follow the trail of the stork its strange
Me missing his track says he
But Im gusseing that bird
Nevar touched this range
For theres no sign of youngsters I see
You bachulars have a joyfull way
When and where ever your found
Forth of July and Paddys day
A Passing the drings around
But to get this joy that Christmas brings
You must be acquanted with three
A homes but a camp with out these things
A Wife the stork and me
And then my bunk pall gives me a shake
An growls in a cranky way
Youv got all the bedding
Im cold as a snake
I wonder what day is today

(Russell verse, 1917)

55

Trail's End

*"The road has been long but my friends
have made it a pleasant one."*

A black hearse drawn by two black horses rolled slowly and silently through the streets of Great Falls. Behind it pranced a big bay horse, its saddle empty and its mane draped in black. The man who once had sat tall in that saddle lay in a coffin in the back of the hearse under a mountain of flowers.

On that late October day in 1926, a hundred automobiles followed the hearse as it wound its way to the cemetery. Throngs of people lined the route, a sprinkle of rain mingling with the tears on their faces. The whole town had closed down for the afternoon. Everyone wanted to pay their respects and say good-bye to their friend, Charlie Russell.

As the hearse passed one of the local schools, a rainbow momentarily arced across the sky. Somehow, it seemed like a fitting tribute to a man who was famous for his masterful use of color.

Hundreds of people turned out for Charlie's funeral procession in 1926. Because he always hated cars and refused ever to drive one, Nancy scoured the countryside for a horse-drawn hearse. The Russell home (at right) and Charlie's log studio still stand in Great Falls, Montana, attracting admirers of the famous Western artist.

C.M. RUSSELL MUSEUM, GREAT FALLS, MONTANA

"The world mourns a great master," the local newspaper said, "but here [in Montana] his genius as an artist yielded to his genius for friendship."

Throughout Charlie's life, friends stuck to him like cockleburs to a coyote. As his fame grew and his frequent travels took him from coast to coast, he began to make the acquaintance of a number of celebrities. Beginning in 1920, the Russells spent their winters in southern California, partly to escape Montana's snow and cold and partly because Charlie's work was popular with the wealthy Hollywood crowd. Soon Charlie counted big-name movie stars among his friends, including Douglas Fairbanks, Bill Hart, Harry Carey, and Will Rogers. He continued to value his old friendships, too, with cowpunchers and Indians.

Charlie invited all his friends to visit him in Great Falls. Sometimes his house bustled like a hotel, as his pals took him up on his offer. Charlie enjoyed cooking for them at the fireplace in his studio. On the menu was an old-fashioned cowboy meal of bacon, beans, and bread. The Russells also entertained guests at a summer cabin they built in what would soon be Glacier National Park.

Charlie's nephew, Austin, spent several summers at the Russell home. As a child, he was more impressed by Charlie's odd habits than by his art. Years later, he recorded this kid's-eye view of his famous uncle:

> He was strange in every way. He wore high-heeled boots, a big hat, no vest—a startling innovation. All the men I knew wore vests even in the St. Louis summer. Instead of suspenders, he held up his pants with a half-breed sash, a Hudson Bay sash, nine feet long. And he didn't tie or buckle it, just tucked it like the latigo on a cinch—give it a jerk in the right direction and it came loose.

Also, he carried no handkerchief. In the morning, he snuffed handfuls of cold water up his nose and snorted it out again—as a horse does at a river on a dusty day—and that sufficed. I tried it faithfully for weeks, but it just wouldn't work; I had to carry a hanky. . . .

Austin also noticed that Charlie had a sweet tooth. He was "like a horse," his nephew said. "The horse eats the oats first and then the hay. If there were cookies on the table, Charlie ate them first; then he didn't want much lunch."

As the Old West faded even farther into history, Charlie was glad to have friends who shared his yearning for the good old days. It grieved him to watch as the West was fenced and plowed in the name of progress.

"Bob, you woldent know the town or the country either," he once wrote to a cowboy friend. "Its all grass side down now. Wher once you rod circle an I night rangled, a gopher couldent graze now. The boosters say its a better country than it ever was, but it looks like hell to me. I liked it better when it belonged to God."

By 1923, Charlie had spent close to sixty years in life's saddle, and he was nearing the end of his trail. He began to suffer from sciatica, a nerve problem that causes pain and weakness in the legs. He grew so stiff and sore that he couldn't climb up or down stairs. In November, he wrote to a friend, "I am better but am still using four legs, the frunt ones are wooden."

Nancy thought the warm California climate might ease Charlie's pain. She suggested that they build a house in Pasadena and live there year-round. To her surprise, Charlie agreed. So in 1926, construction began on an adobe-style house they planned to call Trail's End. Charlie would never get a chance to call the place home.

That spring, Charlie could hardly breathe because of goiter, an enlargement of the thyroid gland that causes swelling in the neck. Nancy begged him to see a doctor, but he refused. He was afraid to have surgery and let some doctor "slit his throat." When he finally agreed to an operation, it was too late. The goiter had damaged his heart, and his doctor predicted he had only months to live.

Charlie died of a heart attack on October 24, 1926, while checking on his sleeping ten-year-old son. He had told Nancy many times that he didn't want to "cross over to the Big Range" in one of those confounded automobiles. He called them "skunk wagons" because of their smelly exhaust, and he had always refused to drive one. To him, they were an unwelcome symbol of the taming of the West. "You can have a car," he once said, "but I'll stick to the hoss; we understan' each other better."

So Nancy searched the county for a horse-drawn hearse. It wasn't easy, but she finally found one in Cascade.

Charlie was buried in Highland Cemetery on the outskirts of Great Falls. His grave overlooks the prairie and mountains he loved for almost fifty years. His passing was mourned by people from all corners of the country. According to one old friend, Charlie "never swung a mean loop in his life, never done dirt to man or animal, in all the days he lived."

Charlie's legacy was a loving look at the untamed West. He captured an important part of our heritage and preserved it through his art. But as his friend Will Rogers pointed out, he left us more than that.

"He not only left us great living Pictures of what our West was," Rogers wrote shortly after Charlie's death, "but he left us an example of how to live in friendship with all mankind. . . . He left us . . . but he *left us much*." ∩

Charles Marion Russell, "Cowboy Artist," 1864-1926.
C.M. RUSSELL MUSEUM, GREAT FALLS, MONTANA

Here's hoping your trail is a long one
Plain and easy to ride
May your dry camps be few
And health ride with you
To the pass on the Big Divide.

C. M. Russell, 1924

Charlie's Country

MONTANA TERRITORY

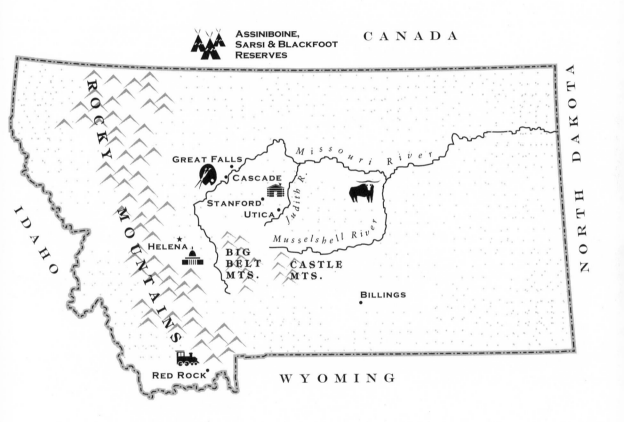

Glossary

Bent's Fort: A fur-trading post built in 1832 on the Santa Fe Trail in what is now Colorado. It was the hub of a trading empire that covered hundreds of square miles of what is now Colorado, Wyoming, Utah, New Mexico, Arizona, Texas, Oklahoma, Kansas, and Nebraska.

buckskin: A soft, tanned leather made from deerskin.

bullwhacker: The person in charge of the oxen teams that pulled heavy freight wagons across the prairies. He walked alongside the wagon and controlled the oxen with a long, rawhide whip.

brand: A mark burned into the hide of an animal with a hot branding iron to indicate who owns it.

bunkhouse: Sleeping quarters for hired hands on a ranch or in a cowboy camp.

chinook: A warm wind that blows down the east side of the Rocky Mountains and causes a sudden rise in temperature.

cowpuncher: A slang term for cowboy.

gelding: A male horse that has been neutered.

greenhorn: A newcomer who is unfamiliar with local ways.

grub: A cowboy's slang term for food.

hide hunter: A person who hunted buffalo to sell their hides. Buffalo robes were very fashionable in the East during the mid-1800s.

lariat: A cowboy's rope, mostly used to capture horses and cattle.

latigo: A leather strap used to fasten the cinch on a saddle.

longhorn: A type of cattle that migrated to the Southwest from Mexico. About five million of them were driven north for shipment to eastern markets or to stock northern ranches. They were named for their huge horns, which could measure six feet from tip to tip.

Louisiana Territory: A region covering approximately the middle third of the continental United States, between the Rocky Mountains and the Mississippi River. France sold the territory to the United States in 1803 for fifteen million dollars. President Thomas Jefferson directed Meriwether Lewis and William Clark to explore it.

masterpiece: An outstanding work of art. Often, an artist's greatest work.

mountain man: In the early 1800s, a man who made his living trapping fur-bearing animals in the western mountains and selling or trading the hides.

mule skinner: A person who drives mule teams.

nighthawk: A person who herds saddle horses at night.

Pony Express: A mail service established in 1860 between St. Joseph, Missouri, and Sacramento, California. Young men on horseback carried the mail in relays. The service lasted a little more than a year.

Rocky Mountain spotted fever: An infectious disease transmitted by ticks. Its symptoms include muscle pains, high fever, and skin eruptions.

riverman: A person, often of French-Canadian descent, who was hired to transport furs and supplies by boat on western rivers.

roundup: The herding of cattle or horses from the open range to a central point for branding, counting, or sorting for shipment to market.

Stetson: A big-brimmed cowboy hat. The original was made by John B. Stetson during an expedition to Pikes Peak in 1863.

trail drive: The moving of cattle via a specific route to a railroad for shipment to eastern markets.

woolly: A western term for a sheep.

wrangler: A person who guarded the extra saddle horses used during roundups and trail drives. He also was responsible for catching the horses when the cowboys wanted to change mounts. Each cowboy usually had five to nine extra horses. When one got tired, he traded it for another. A nighthawk is also a wrangler.

yarn: A long, complicated story about real or imaginary adventures, often elaborated upon by the teller.

Bibliography

Broderick, Janice K. *Charles M. Russell: American Artist.*
St. Louis, Mo.: Jefferson National Expansion Historical
Association, 1982.

Dear, Elizabeth. *Regards to the Bunch: Letters, Poems, and Illustrations of C. M. Russell.* Great Falls, Mont.: C.M. Russell
Museum, 1992.

Dippie, Brian W., ed. *Charles M. Russell, Word Painter.* Fort
Worth, Tex.: Amon Carter Museum, 1993.

Hassrick, Peter H. *Charles M. Russell.* New York: Harry N.
Abrams Inc. in association with National Museum of American Art, Smithsonian Institution, 1989.

Howard, Joseph Kinsey. *Montana: High, Wide, and Handsome.*
1959. Reprint, Lincoln: Univ. of Nebraska Press, 1983.

Linderman, Frank Bird. *Recollections of Charley Russell.* Norman:
Univ. of Oklahoma Press, 1963.

Malone, Michael P., and Richard B. Roeder. *Montana: A History
of Two Centuries.* Seattle: Univ. of Washington Press, 1976.

McCracken, Harold. *The Charles M. Russell Book.* Garden City,
N.Y.: Doubleday & Co., 1957.

"Montana Mourns at Charlie Russell's Grave." *Great Falls
Tribune*, 28, October 1926.

A Portrait of Charles M. Russell: Preserver of the Old West. Seattle: High Hopes Production, 1993. Videotape.

Renner, Frederic G. *Charles M. Russell*. 1966. Reprint, New York: Abradale Press/Harry N. Abrams Inc. in association with Amon Carter Museum of Western Art, 1984.

Renner, Ginger K. "Charlie and the Ladies in His Life." *Montana, the Magazine of Western History*, Summer 1984.

Russell, Austin. *Charles M. Russell, Cowboy Artist*. New York: Twayne Publishers, 1957.

Russell, C. M. "Charlie Tells His Own Story." *Persimmon Hill 2*, nos. 3 and 4. First published in *Butte (Mont.) Intermountain*, 1 January 1903.

——. *More Rawhides*. 1925. Reprint, Pasadena, Calif.: Trail's End Publishing Co., 1946.

——. *Paper Talk: Illustrated Letters of Charles M. Russell*. Fort Worth, Tex.: Amon Carter Museum of Western Art, 1962.

——. *Trails Plowed Under*. Reprint, New York: Doubleday, Doran & Co., 1944.

Russell, Nancy, ed. *Good Medicine: The Illustrated Letters of Charles M. Russell*. Garden City, N.Y.: Doubleday & Co., 1929.

Shirley, Gayle C. "Nancy Cooper Russell: Woman Behind the Man." In *More Than Petticoats: Remarkable Montana Women*. Helena, Mont.: Falcon Press, 1995.

Stauffer, Joan. *Behind Every Man: The Story of Nancy Cooper Russell*. Tulsa, Okla.: Daljo Publishing, 1990.

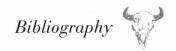

Stewart, Rick. *Charles M. Russell, Sculptor*. Fort Worth, Tex.:
Amon Carter Museum, 1994.

Warden, R. D. *C. M. Russell Boyhood Sketchbook*. Bozeman,
Mont.: Treasure Products, 1972.

Index

About the Author

Gayle C. Shirley has written eight other nonfiction books for children and young adults, including *M is for Montana*, *Montana Wildlife*, and *More than Petticoats: Remarkable Montana Women*. She is the author of a series of books about animal legends from throughout the West.

Gayle grew up in Colorado and Idaho but moved to the Treasure State to attend the University of Montana. She graduated in 1978 with a degree in journalism and worked for two daily newspapers before writing her first book. She now devotes her time to freelance writing and editing. In addition to her books, she has written articles for magazines such as *Boy's Life* and *Falcon*. She lives with her husband, Steve, and sons, Colin and Jesse, in Great Falls, Montana. ∩

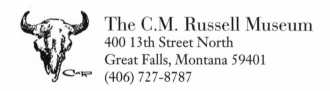

The C.M. Russell Museum
400 13th Street North
Great Falls, Montana 59401
(406) 727-8787

The C.M. Russell Museum is dedicated to the interpretation and preservation of the work and life of Charles M. Russell, and to sharing his unique art and vision with the people who love the West as Charlie did. The Museum houses Russell's work and owns and is located on the same block as his home and the log studio in which he finished all of his art works after 1903. Russell completed approximately 4,500 works of art during his lifetime, and the C.M. Russell Museum owns the most complete collection of his works and memorabilia in the world. The C.M. Russell Museum is, indeed, a living museum for a legendary man. ∩